Battles of the Spanish-American War

Diane Smolinski

Series Consultant:
Lieutenant Colonel G.A. LoFaro

Heinemann Library
Chicago, Illinois

Designed by Herman Adler Design
Photo research by Julie Laffin
Printed and bound in the United States by Lake Book
Manufacturing, Inc.

07 06 05 04 03
10 9 8 7 6 5 4 3 2 1

Library of Congress Cataloging-in-Publication Data
Smolinski, Diane, 1950-
   Battles of the Spanish-American War / Diane
Smolinski.
      v. cm. -- (Americans at war. The Spanish-
American War)
Includes bibliographical references and index.
Contents: Influence of newspapers -- President
William McKinley -- The USS Maine -- The U.S.
prepares for war -- Spain prepares for war -- The
Caribbean campaign -- Battle of El Caney, -- San Juan
Heights -- Puerto Rico -- U.S. troops land in Puerto
Rico -- The Pacific campaign -- Battle of Manila Bay --
Treaty of Paris -- After the war.
   ISBN 1-4034-0170-5
   1. Spanish-American War, 1898--Campaigns--Juvenile
literature. [1. Spanish-American War, 1898--
Campaigns.] I. Title.
   E717 .S63 2002
   973.8'93--dc21
                                     2002005085

Acknowledgments
The author and publishers are grateful to the following
for permission to reproduce copyright material:
Contents page, pp. 17, 20B Mary Evans Picture
Library; pp. 5, 6, 8, 9, 12, 24B, 26 Bettmann/Corbis;
pp. 7, 10, 11, 16, 18, 20T, 25 The Granger Collection,
New York; p. 13 North Wind Picture Archives; pp. 14,
23 Library of Congress; p. 15 Bryan Knox/Corbis; p.
21 Dave G. Houser/Corbis; p. 24T Brown Brothers;
pp. 28, 29 Corbis.

Cover photographs: (main) The Granger Collection,
New York, (border, T-B) Philip James Corwin/Corbis,
Reuters NewMedia Inc./Corbis.

Every effort has been made to contact copyright
holders of any material reproduced in this book. Any
omissions will be rectified in subsequent printings if
notice is given to the publisher.

About the Author
Diane Smolinski is the author of two previous series
of books on the Revolutionary and Civil Wars. She
earned degrees in education from Duquesne and
Slippery Rock Universities and taught in public
schools for 28 years. Diane now writes for teachers,
helping them to use nonfiction books in their
classrooms. She currently lives in Florida with her
husband, Henry, and their cat, Pepper.

Special thanks to Lt. Colonel Guy LoFaro for his
interest and expertise in military history. May all
young readers be inspired by his passion for history to
extend their learning well beyond the words written
on these pages.

About the Consultant
G.A. LoFaro is a lieutenant colonel in the U.S. Army
currently stationed at Fort McPherson, Georgia. After
graduating from West Point, he was commissioned in
the infantry. He has served in a variety of positions in
the 82nd Airborne Division, the Ranger Training
Brigade, and Second Infantry Division in Korea.
He has a Masters Degree in U.S. History from the
University of Michigan and is completing his Ph.D in
U.S. History at the State University of New York at
Stony Brook. He has also served six years on the West
Point faculty where he taught military history to cadets.

On the cover: This lithograph depicts American troops charging at San Juan Hill, Cuba, on July 1, 1898.
On the contents page: This sketch shows the Battle of El Caney. Under General Shafter, 12,000 Americans took San Juan Hill despite fierce resistance from the Spanish.

Some words are shown in bold, **like this.**
You can find out what they mean by looking in the glossary.

Contents

11/2003
Rainbow
$17 95

Battles of the Spanish-American War

In the 1890s, many European countries possessed colonies throughout the world. The islands of Cuba, Puerto Rico, and the Philippines were colonies that belonged to the country of Spain. In 1898, the United States became more involved in world politics by helping these colonies gain independence from Spain.

Almost immediately, the United States had an interest in the island nation of Cuba. Since 1511, Cuba had been primarily under Spanish rule. Located only 90 miles (145 kilometers) from the United States, many U.S. businessmen owned land in Cuba where sugar and tobacco was grown. They wanted to protect these business interests.

Spain is located over 4,500 miles (7,242 kilometers) from Cuba, over 7,000 miles (11,265 kilometers) from the Philippines, and about 3,900 miles (6,276 kilometers) from Puerto Rico. The great distances made it hard for Spain to rule over their colonies.

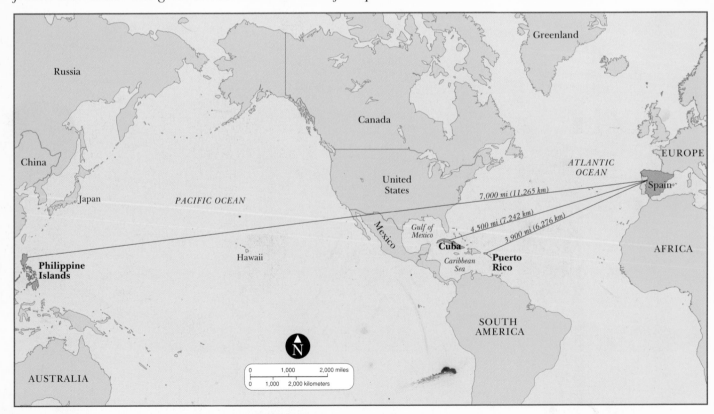

These United States' businessmen became concerned that they would lose much money if the Spanish continued to control Cuba. Also, some people believed the Spanish treated the native Cubans unfairly, placing them in "reconcentration" camps. These people pressured the United States government into helping the Cubans.

The United States declared war on Spain in April of 1898, after peaceful attempts to settle their differences about issues in Cuba failed. The Spanish-American War was fought in two different parts of the world. Most of the battles occurred in the **Caribbean** around the island of Cuba. Other fighting took place in the Pacific Ocean around the islands of the Philippines.

The battles discussed here represent significant happenings on both the Caribbean and Pacific **fronts,** ending centuries of Spanish control over Cuba, Puerto Rico, and the Philippines.

On August 19, 1898, Spanish troops left Mayagues, Puerto Rico, to meet U.S. troops at Hormiguero. By October, all Spanish troops had left Puerto Rico and returned to Spain, defeated.

Influence of Newspapers

Before the Spanish-American War began, two newspaper owners competed for business in New York City. William Randolph Hearst owned the *New York Journal*, and Joseph Pulitzer owned the *New York World*.

A Newspaper War

In 1898, people depended on newspapers for information about world events. Americans were interested in the disagreements between the United States and Spain over Cuba. The newspapers reported all the details. People eagerly bought these newspapers, and both Hearst and Pulitzer profited from increased sales.

Yellow Journalism

Newspapers influenced the thoughts and opinions of Americans before and during the Spanish-American War. Too often, though, the facts were reported inaccurately or were exaggerated. For example, the Spanish were only described as being cruel toward the Cubans. This "yellow journalism," as these exaggerations became called, helped to sell newspapers during these emotional times.

In 1898, crowds often gathered outside the offices of the New York Journal *to read the latest news posted on boards.*

1898 Gazette

- "Yellow journalism" got its name from a comic strip character, *The Yellow Kid,* by R.F. Outcault. It appeared in the New York newspapers of both William Randolph Hearst and Joseph Pulitzer from 1895 to 1898. Bright yellow ink was used to color the Yellow Kid's nightshirt in order to attract readers to the newspapers. From this time, the term "yellow journalism" continues to mean using sensational ways to catch the attention of and influence readers.

- William Randolph Hearst inherited his first newspaper from his father. He made this small newspaper business grow into a fortune by expanding into the magazine, radio, and movie newsreel businesses.

- Joseph Pulitzer, an immigrant from Hungary, worked for newspapers. He then bought his first of many newspapers. Since 1917, awards called Pulitzer Prizes are given each year for excellence in writing.

The de Lôme Letter

Early in 1898, Enrique Dupuy de Lôme, the Spanish Minister to the United States, wrote a letter to a friend in Cuba. Part of this letter criticized the leadership of the current United States president, William McKinley. This letter was **intercepted** and given to William Randolph Hearst's *New York Journal*. It was printed on February 9, 1898 with spectacular headlines. At a time when many Americans wanted the United States government to take action against the Spanish government, this letter caused even stronger feelings against Spain.

1898 Gazette

De Lôme wrote the following in his now infamous letter, criticizing President McKinley:

*...it shows once more what McKinley is: weak and catering to the rabble, and, besides, a low politician, who desires to leave a door open to me and to stand well with the **jingoes** of his party.*

The front page of the New York Journal on March 29, 1898, featured headlines criticizing Spain, while encouraging the U.S. to support the Cubans.

President William McKinley (1843–1901)

Before becoming president of the United States, William McKinley was a teacher, a lawyer, a soldier who fought on the side of the Union in the **Civil War,** a member of the U.S. House of Representatives, and governor of Ohio. In 1901, shortly after beginning his second term as president, William McKinley was assassinated.

Many people were critical of McKinley's handling of policies during the Spanish-American War. They felt that the newspapers and other **political** figures pressured him into declaring war on Spain. The lands that were acquired from the war under his administration, however, did allow the United States to become and remain a significant world power.

President McKinley saw how war could devastate a country during the Civil War. He tried hard to find a peaceful way to settle the differences between the U.S. and Spain in 1898.

1898 Gazette

William McKinley beat the same opponent, William Jennings Bryan, twice for the presidency.

1898	FEBRUARY	APRIL	MAY	JUNE

2/15 Sinking of the USS *Maine*

The USS *Maine*

In 1898, the Spanish government refused to give up control of the island of Cuba to the Cuban people. Political relationships between the United States and Spain worsened over issues about the control of Cuba. The United States Navy anchored a battleship, the USS *Maine*, in Havana Harbor to help calm fears about the safety of U.S. citizens in Cuba.

1898 Gazette

- The commander of the USS *Maine* was Captain Charles Dwight Sigsbee. Since his quarters were in the back part of the ship, he survived.

- There were 266 casualties reported after the explosion.

On the evening of February 15, 1898 at 9:40 p.m., the USS *Maine* exploded and sank in Havana Harbor. This explosion occurred in the front part of the ship, where much of the gunpowder was stored and where the enlisted men slept.

The USS Maine, *shown here in Havana Harbor in January 1898, was a 6,682-ton second-class battleship. It was built at the New York Navy Yard and put into service in September of 1895.*

JULY   OCTOBER   DECEMBER

What Caused the Explosion?

At first, many Americans blamed Spain for the explosion of the USS *Maine*. They suspected that the Spanish set a mine or launched a torpedo. The Spanish government claimed no fault for the tragedy. Some Americans did believe it was an accident. They believed that burning coal in the ship's boiler probably caught fire and caused the gunpowder to explode.

In 1898, a team of Navy investigators reported that a mine caused the explosion, but did not blame a specific country. Even today, no one agrees on a definite cause.

Yellow Journalism

The newspapers reported the explosion in a sensational manner, blaming Spain. Many Americans believed the newspaper reports and were angry at Spain. More than ever, they wanted the United States to help the Cubans gain their independence from Spanish rule.

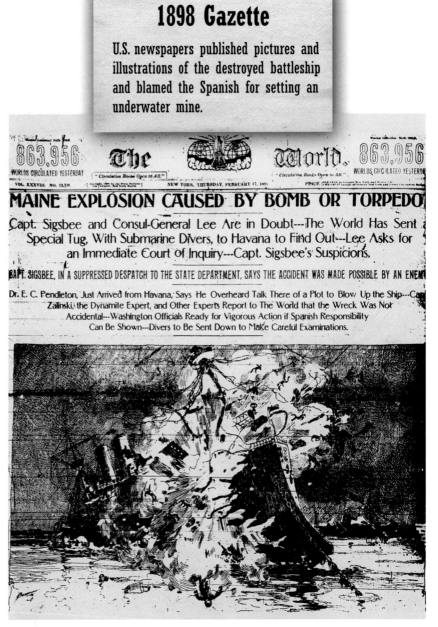

1898 Gazette

U.S. newspapers published pictures and illustrations of the destroyed battleship and blamed the Spanish for setting an underwater mine.

Spectacular headlines and illustrations, like that shown above, caused strong feelings against the Spanish occupation of Cuba.

1898 ▶ **FEBRUARY**   **APRIL**   **MAY**   **JUNE**

2/15 Sinking of the USS *Maine*

4/21 U.S. Navy begins blockade of Cuba
4/23 Spain declares war on the U.S.
4/25 U.S. declares war on Spain

The relationship between the United States and Spain over affairs in Cuba were strained even before war was officially declared. On March 8, 1898, Congress voted to create a war fund of $50 million. All U.S. citizens were moved from Cuba in early April of 1898. Within a few weeks, war was declared.

No Compromise

President McKinley supported the idea that the Cuban people should be free. He tried to convince the Spanish and Cubans to settle their differences in a peaceful manner. Spain would not agree to leave Cuba. The United States prepared for war against Spain.

Declaration of War

On the morning of April 19, 1898, **Congress** passed and President McKinley signed a **resolution** that stated:

…the government of the U.S. does hereby demand that the government of Spain at once relinquish its authority and government in the island of Cuba, and withdraw its land and naval **forces** from Cuba and Cuban waters.

Spain still did not leave Cuba. On April 21, 1898, the United States Navy received orders to **blockade** the waters around Cuba. Two days later, Spain declared war.

On April 25, 1898, the United States Congress officially declared war on Spain.

1898 Gazette

- As part of the blockade, the U.S. Navy positioned battleships, armored cruisers, monitors, and other small vessels around the island of Cuba.

- Battleships at this time were often named after states of the Union. For example, the USS *Indiana,* the USS *Massachusetts,* the USS *Oregon,* the USS *Iowa,* and the USS *Texas* were part of the American **fleet.**

The U.S. Prepares for War

The U.S. Navy blockaded the ports around Cuba. Spanish forces on the island could not leave, nor could troops pass the blockade to help Spain defend the island.

The United States government was not ready for war. Even though men volunteered for military duty, money was needed to provide training, weapons, and equipment for the volunteers. Ships were also needed to transport the additional troops and supplies to Cuba.

While the United States prepared to send troops to Cuba, the U.S. Navy fought and destroyed Spanish ships at the Battle of Manila Bay near the Philippine Islands in the Pacific Ocean. This prevented Spanish ships in the Pacific from sailing to help their troops in Cuba.

The U.S. Navy, unlike other parts of the U.S. government, was actually ready for war in 1898. So when war broke out, the Navy was well-prepared to take on and defeat the Spanish fleets, as well as to transport troops to wherever they were needed.

1898 Gazette

- Rear Admiral William T. Sampson commanded the U.S. Navy fleet in the **Caribbean.**

- General William R. Shafter was the U.S. Army commander for the Caribbean **Campaign** in Cuba.

1898	FEBRUARY	APRIL	MAY	JUNE
	2/15 Sinking of the USS *Maine*	4/21 U.S. Navy begins blockade of Cuba 4/23 Spain declares war on the U.S. 4/25 U.S. declares war on Spain	5/1 Battle of Manila Bay	

Spain Prepares for War

Admiral Pascual Cervera y Topete sailed a small fleet from Spain to the Caribbean in April 1898. People in American cities along the east coast became worried when they found out the Spanish Navy was crossing the Atlantic Ocean.

Cervera needed coal to refuel his ships. He discovered that the U.S. Navy was not guarding the port of Santiago de Cuba. He planned to quickly refuel and leave. Once the U.S. Navy realized Cervera was in Cuba, they blockaded Santiago **Harbor** so his ships could not leave.

The United States moved troops and ships in position to drive the Spanish from the city of Santiago de Cuba.

1898 Gazette

- Admiral Pascual Cervera was the commander of the Spanish Navy in the Caribbean.

- General Arsenio Linares was the Spanish commander in Cuba.

The U.S. Navy positioned eleven warships outside the harbor of Santiago de Cuba. Six Spanish warships were trapped inside the harbor.

JULY   OCTOBER   DECEMBER

13

The Caribbean Campaign

Santiago, Cuba
June/July 1898

Even though the United States Navy had the Spanish **fleet** trapped in Santiago **Harbor, shore batteries** protected Santiago, keeping enemy ships from entering the harbor to attack the city. Army troops were needed to help capture these shore batteries.

Daiquiri, Cuba
June 22, 1898

To avoid the shore batteries around Santiago, U.S. Navy ships carried army troops to a city named Daiquiri, about twenty miles (32 kilometers) east of Santiago. In two days, more than 15,000 U.S. troops went ashore in small boats. Their mules and horses had to swim. Many animals died.

Cuban troops helped the U.S. Army attack the Spanish **forces.** Once U.S. Navy ships began bombarding Daiquiri, Spanish troops abandoned the city. The U.S. captured the city without a fight.

Shore batteries such as these were used to protect important harbors and cities.

1898 Gazette

Daiquiri was used as a **supply depot** to store ammunition, food, mules, wagons, and other supplies for the U.S. troops during the Santiago **campaign.**

After Action Report—Daiquiri

	United States	Spain
Commanders	General William R. Shafter	General Arsenio Linares
Casualties	0	0
Outcome	victory	defeat

1898	FEBRUARY	APRIL	MAY	JUNE
	2/15 Sinking of the USS *Maine*	**4/21** U.S. Navy begins blockade of Cuba **4/23** Spain declares war on the U.S. **4/25** U.S. declares war on Spain	**5/1** Battle of Manila Bay	**6/22** First landing of U.S. troops at Daiquiri, Cuba **6/22** Capture of Siboney, Cuba

As U.S. troops fought the Spanish fleet, they slowly moved westward along the southern coast of Cuba until they reached the city of Santiago.

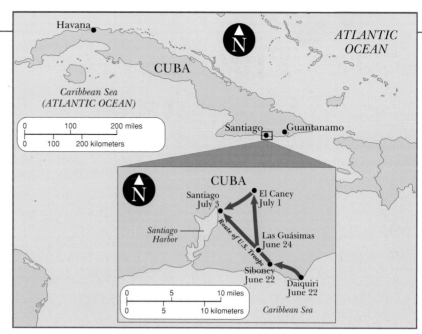

Siboney, Cuba
June 22, 1898

After U.S. troops landed at Daiquiri, some were sent to capture the town of Siboney. Being closer to Santiago, the U.S. continued to use this port city to land troops and supplies throughout the Santiago campaign.

From Siboney, U.S. troops continued to move toward Santiago. Due to the lack of supplies and poor roads, the march was slow and difficult. The hot, humid weather exhausted the men and caused illnesses such as **malaria.**

At the same time, U.S. Navy ships carefully watched the Spanish fleet in Santiago Harbor. Admiral Cervera knew he had little food and ammunition, but he could not get past the U.S. Navy fleet blocking the entrance to the harbor.

1898 Gazette

More men died from tropical diseases than bullets during the Spanish-American War. Malaria took the most lives. People get malaria when they are bitten by certain kinds of mosquitoes that carry the disease. A high fever of 105°F (41°C), a bad headache, a swollen tongue and face, and difficulty sleeping are all symptoms of the disease.

The jungle-like conditions in Cuba made traveling by land very difficult for U.S. troops. Often, they had to travel through areas with no roads at all.

JULY   OCTOBER   DECEMBER

Las Guásimas, Cuba
June 24, 1898

U.S. troops fought their first battle against the Spanish Army two days later. U.S. **infantry** and **cavalry** soldiers met about 1,500 Spanish soldiers waiting in the hills near the town of Las Guásimas. Jungle growth hid the Spanish soldiers.

The Spanish Army was able to delay U.S. troops because they were more familiar with the local, hilly terrain and jungle conditions in Cuba.

As the U.S. troops approached, the Spanish soldiers began to fire. U.S. troops formed a line and moved toward the hills. Firing their weapons, they kept moving forward toward the Spanish at the top of the hills. The Spanish returned fire from atop the hills. After about two hours of battle, the Spanish left the hills and returned to Santiago. U.S. troops did not follow. They had captured the hills.

U.S. troops rested and re-supplied before moving closer to Santiago.

After Action Report

	United States	Spain
Commanders	General Samuel M.B. Young	General Antero Rubín
Casualties	16 killed, 52 wounded	10 killed, 25 wounded
Outcome	victory	defeat

1898

FEBRUARY	APRIL	MAY	JUNE
2/15 Sinking of the USS *Maine*	**4/21** U.S. Navy begins blockade of Cuba **4/23** Spain declares war on the U.S. **4/25** U.S. declares war on Spain	**5/1** Battle of Manila Bay	**6/22** First landing of U.S. troops at Daiquiri, Cuba **6/22** Capture of Siboney, Cuba **6/24** Battle at Las Guásimas, Cuba

The Battle of El Caney

General Lawton led U.S. troops toward a Spanish-held village named El Caney. It was important for the U.S. to capture this village because it supplied water to Santiago. General Linares positioned more than 10,000 Spanish troops on the hills and in nearby towns surrounding Santiago. The Spanish were ready for an attack. Cuban citizens blocked the road between Santiago and El Caney to keep Spanish **reinforcements** from going to El Caney to help.

1898 Gazette

About 520 Spanish soldiers held their position for almost eight hours against about 5,400 U.S. troops.

U.S. troops used artillery to help them defeat Spanish troops that were **entrenched** *in hilltop positions.*

Exchange of Fire

The U.S. attacked with light **artillery** and infantry. Spanish and U.S. soldiers exchanged fire for nearly eight hours. At the height of the battle, U.S. artillery directed its fire at the small Spanish stone fort, El Viso. The U.S. infantry stormed and controlled the fort. The Spanish retreated to Santiago.

The U.S. would now move toward the San Juan Heights, a well-**fortified** area.

After Action Report

	United States	Spain
Commanders	General Henry W. Lawton	General Arsenio Linares
Casualties	81 killed, 360 wounded	about 235 killed or wounded
Outcome	victory	defeat

JULY   **OCTOBER**   **DECEMBER**

San Juan Heights

Approximately 500 Spanish soldiers were entrenched on the hills of the San Juan Heights. Protected by barbed wire, they waited for the approaching U.S. Army troops.

Early in the morning on July 1, 1898, General Sumner's **brigade** marched down the main road toward Santiago. Once they were in range, the U.S. fired **artillery** at the Heights. Now knowing the location of the U.S. troops, the Spanish returned fire, destroying U.S. artillery protection.

San Juan Hill
July 1, 1898

The 71st New York Volunteers attacked the Heights first. Spanish soldiers fired from atop San Juan Hill. The volunteers turned back. Other U.S. Army units tried to attack the hill. The determined Spanish troops held their ground, causing many U.S. casualties.

*Fourteen **Medals of Honor** were awarded to U.S. soldiers for bravery during the Battles of San Juan and Kettle Hills.*

1898	FEBRUARY	APRIL	MAY	JUNE
	2/15 Sinking of the USS *Maine*	4/21 U.S. Navy begins blockade of Cuba 4/23 Spain declares war on the U.S. 4/25 U.S. declares war on Spain	5/1 Battle of Manila Bay	6/22 First landing of U.S. troops at Daiquiri, Cuba 6/22 Capture of Siboney, Cuba 6/24 Battle at Las Guásimas, Cuba

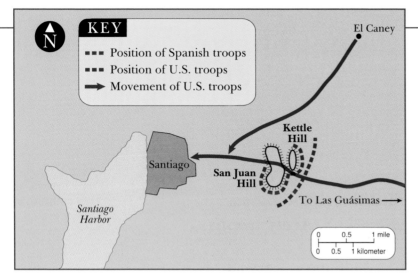

The San Juan Heights, which includes San Juan and Kettle Hills, are a group of hills that surround the city of Santiago, Cuba. The Spanish chose this high ground as the site from which to defend this important seaport city.

Kettle Hill
July 1, 1898

While soldiers fought to take San Juan Hill, African-American troops of the U.S. Army 9th **Cavalry** led the attack on Kettle Hill. The 1st Cavalry and the Rough Riders followed. As the troops neared the top, the Spanish left the hill. U.S. troops now turned their attention to San Juan Hill. They fired on it from Kettle Hill.

The Rough Riders moved back toward San Juan Hill. In less than one hour, U.S. troops controlled both San Juan and Kettle Hills. The U.S. did not follow the Spanish. They stayed on the hills to protect their position from a **counterattack.** The Spanish did not return, but continued to Santiago to join Spanish soldiers defending the city.

1898 Gazette

The men of the 1st Volunteer Cavalry unit that fought in the Spanish-American War named themselves the "Rough Riders." They trained in San Antonio, Texas, and then boarded ships in Tampa, Florida, for Cuba. Colonel Leonard Wood, a medical doctor who was well known for fighting battles against the Indians in the western United States, was appointed the commander. Theodore Roosevelt, a future president of the United States, was second in command of the unit. Wood was promoted before the Battle of Kettle Hill, so Lt. Colonel Roosevelt was in command of the Rough Riders that day.

After Action Report

	United States	Spain
Commanders	General William R. Shafter	General Arsenio Linares General Jose Toral (took over after Linares was killed)
Casualties	205 killed, 1,180 wounded	358 killed or wounded
Outcome	victory	defeat

JULY	OCTOBER	DECEMBER

7/1 Battle of San Juan Hill
7/1 Battle of Kettle Hill

The Spanish squadron in Santiago Harbor was outnumbered and unable to get supplies and ammunition. As a result, the U.S. Navy easily defeated it.

What Next?

General Shafter prepared to attack the city of Santiago. Shafter asked the U.S. Navy to help by sailing into Santiago **Harbor.** Admiral Sampson wanted the army to first destroy Spanish **shore batteries.** Before they reached a decision, the Spanish made a surprise move.

1898 Gazette

It only took the U.S. Navy four hours to destroy the Spanish fleet in Santiago Harbor.

Santiago Abandoned
July 3, 1898

Admiral Cervera received orders from Spain to leave Santiago Harbor. His **fleet** was destroyed as it tried to leave the harbor. With the Spanish fleet gone, the U.S. Navy bombarded the city of Santiago. The Spanish commander surrendered. U.S. troops entered Santiago to keep order until the Spanish Army left Cuba.

U.S. **forces** would now go to Puerto Rico, another island nation in the **Caribbean** under Spanish control.

Buglers play as the Spanish Army officially surrenders the city of Santiago.

1898	FEBRUARY	APRIL	MAY	JUNE
	2/15 Sinking of the USS *Maine*	4/21 U.S. Navy begins blockade of Cuba 4/23 Spain declares war on the U.S. 4/25 U.S. declares war on Spain	5/1 Battle of Manila Bay	6/22 First landing of U.S. troops at Daiquiri, Cuba 6/22 Capture of Siboney, Cuba 6/24 Battle at Las Guásimas, Cuba

Puerto Rico

In 1898, the island of Puerto Rico was a Spanish-held colony. Puerto Ricans wanted to be free from Spanish control. The United States would help them win this freedom.

> ## 1898 Gazette
> Admiral William T. Sampson was the commander of the U.S. Navy ships at Puerto Rico.

In May 1898, fighting began on the island of Puerto Rico between Spain and the United States. U.S. Navy ships sailed into the harbor at San Juan and exchanged cannon fire with Spanish **land batteries.** For the next few days, U.S. Navy ships bombarded the city of San Juan. They then **blockaded** San Juan Harbor, preventing supplies and troops from coming to help the Spanish.

In July, 3,300 U.S. troops were transported from Cuba to the southern coast of Puerto Rico to help the U.S. gain control of the island.

When the U.S. arrived in Puerto Rico, Spanish troops were positioned at the Fortress San Cristobal. From there, they could see who was arriving and leaving San Juan Harbor.

JULY	OCTOBER	DECEMBER
7/1 Battle of San Juan Hill		
7/1 Battle of Kettle Hill		
7/3 Battle of Santiago		

U.S. Troops Land in Puerto Rico

U.S. troops first landed at Guánica, a city on the southern coast of Puerto Rico, on July 25, 1898. The main road from Guánica led to Ponce, the largest city in Puerto Rico at this time. U.S. troops moved north and east toward Ponce, fighting small battles along the way. By the time U.S. troops reached Ponce, the regular Spanish **forces** had already left.

Throughout the war, U.S. **cavalry, infantry,** and **artillery** troops came onto the island at Guánica, Playa de Ponce, and Arroyo. All were ideal seaports for U.S. troops and supplies to come onto the island.

U.S. General Miles now planned to capture San Juan, a city on the northern coast of Puerto Rico.

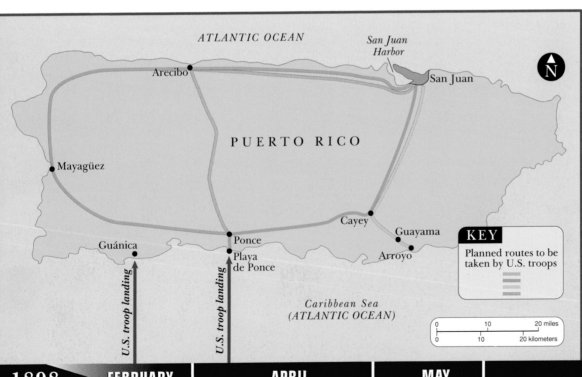

U.S. troops did not meet many enemy troops as they landed at seaports along the southern coast of Puerto Rico.

1898	FEBRUARY	APRIL	MAY	JUNE
	2/15 Sinking of the USS *Maine*	4/21 U.S. Navy begins blockade of Cuba 4/23 Spain declares war on the U.S. 4/25 U.S. declares war on Spain	5/1 Battle of Manila Bay	6/22 First landing of U.S. troops at Daiquiri, Cuba 6/22 Capture of Siboney, Cuba 6/24 Battle at Las Guásimas, Cuba

Moving Toward San Juan

General Miles mapped out his strategy. He planned to send forces to the west and north, capturing the cities of Mayagüez and Arecibo. These forces would meet at Arecibo and go east to capture San Juan. Other forces would take a more easterly route. Leaving Ponce and Guayama, they would meet in Cayey. Both forces would then continue north to San Juan. The U.S. Navy would be waiting in San Juan **Harbor** to help.

As U.S. troops advanced toward San Juan, the Spanish retreated into the mountains. Battles were fought in many cities along the way, all ending in U.S. victories. Before U.S. troops even reached San Juan, the war had ended. Puerto Rico would now be under a U.S. military government until 1900.

On September 9, 1898, United States and Spanish government representatives met in San Juan, Puerto Rico. They decided that Spanish troops would leave the island and Puerto Rico would come under U.S. control. On October 18, 1898, all Spanish troops left San Juan for Spain.

1898 Gazette

- San Juan is the capital city of Puerto Rico.

- Poor roads, mountainous terrain, diseases caused by the tropical climate, and unhealthy conditions slowed the U.S. advance to San Juan.

JULY	OCTOBER	DECEMBER
7/1 Battle of San Juan Hill 7/1 Battle of Kettle Hill 7/3 Battle of Santiago 7/25 U.S. troops land in Puerto Rico	10/18 Last Spanish troops leave Puerto Rico	

The Pacific Campaign

The United States Navy Prepares for War

The United States Navy kept **fleets** in the Atlantic and Pacific Oceans to protect the country. In April 1898, the Atlantic fleet was on its way to **blockade** Cuba. Commodore Dewey now prepared his **Asiatic Squadron** for war. The men practiced battle **maneuvers** such as firing cannons and sailing their ships. Repairs were made so that ships would be in good working condition.

On April 25, 1898, Dewey received orders from officials in Washington, D.C. that stated:

> War has commenced between the United States and Spain. Proceed at once, particularly against Spanish fleet. You must capture vessels or destroy…

U.S. Navy warships would sail 620 miles (998 kilometers) to reach the Spanish fleet in the Philippines. It was important that no Spanish warships leave the Pacific to aid the Spanish Army in Cuba.

Commodore George Dewey commanded the U.S. Asiatic Squadron in the Pacific. His flagship, right, was named the USS Olympia.

Commodore George Dewey 1837–1917

- Dewey graduated from the U.S. Naval Academy in 1857.
- In 1897, he was named commander of the Asiatic Squadron, part of the U.S. Navy assigned to the Pacific Ocean.
- In 1899, **Congress** appointed Dewey Admiral of the Navy.
- George Dewey served in the U.S. Navy until his death at age 79.

Admiral Patricio Montojo y Pasarón 1839–1917

- In 1852, Montojo became a naval cadet at the Naval School in Cadiz, Spain.
- From 1855 until after the Battle of Manila Bay in 1898, he served in many parts of the world for the Spanish Navy.
- While serving in the Philippines in 1898, Montojo was the general commander of all the naval stations in those islands.
- Because of the loss of his squadron at Manila Bay, Montojo was sent to Spain where he was discharged from the Spanish Navy.

The Spanish Navy Prepares for War

The Philippine Islands were an important Spanish **colony.** Once war was declared between the U.S. and Spain, the Spanish fleet, based in Manila Bay, prepared a defense. They positioned **shore batteries** and set floating mines to protect the entrance to the bay. The Spanish also had the advantage of being familiar with the waters around Manila Bay. The U.S. had to rely on information provided by merchant ships, since their Navy vessels had not sailed in these waters for almost twenty years. A disadvantage for the Spanish was that all their ships were made of wood. They would be fighting U.S. ships made of iron.

On April 28, 1898, Admiral Montojo learned that Commodore Dewey's squadron was sailing toward the Philippines. In just three days, these two navies would meet in battle at Manila Bay.

Admiral Patricio Montojo y Pasarón commanded the Spanish fleet in the Philippines. His flagship was named the Reina Cristina.

The Battle of Manila Bay

You may fire when ready, Gridley.
—**Commodore George Dewey**

On the evening of April 30, 1898, Commodore George Dewey sailed his squadron of six ships into Manila Bay. Spanish **shore batteries** fired, but they caused no damage to the U.S. ships. U.S. Navy ships looked for the Spanish ships waiting in the **harbor.**

Early the next morning, as the U.S. ships moved through Manila Bay, they found the Spanish **fleet** anchored off the shore of Cavite. Spanish ships and shore batteries fired, doing little damage to the U.S. ships. Spanish ships stayed in the harbor while the U.S. ships passed back and forth. Admiral Montojo moved his **flagship,** the *Reina Cristina*, out to attack the USS *Olympia*. Dewey ordered the captain of his flagship to "fire when ready." The *Reina Cristina* was badly damaged.

The destruction of the Spanish fleet by the U.S. Navy at Manila Bay prevented the Spanish ships from sailing to help the war effort in Cuba.

1898 Gazette

- *USS* before a ship's name stands for United States Ship.

- Captain Charles Vernon Gridley (1844–1898) graduated from the U.S. Naval Academy at Annapolis, Maryland, in 1864. He first served in the U.S. Navy during the American **Civil War.**

1898	FEBRUARY	APRIL	MAY	JUNE
	2/15 Sinking of the USS *Maine*	**4/21** U.S. Navy begins blockade of Cuba **4/23** Spain declares war on the U.S. **4/25** U.S. declares war on Spain	**5/1** Battle of Manila Bay	**6/22** First landing of U.S. troops at Daiquiri, Cuba **6/22** Capture of Siboney, Cuba **6/24** Battle at Las Guásimas, Cuba

When war was declared, the U.S. Pacific Fleet was in China. It quickly set sail for the Philippine Islands to meet the Spanish fleet.

The entire Spanish fleet suffered much damage. Realizing they were defeated, Admiral Montojo ordered his men to sink their ships before surrendering to the U.S.

Commodore Dewey threatened to bombard the city of Manila if the shelling from the shore batteries did not stop. The shelling stopped, and within six hours the entire Spanish fleet was destroyed. The U.S. Navy controlled the ocean around the Philippines. Their defeat of the Spanish fleet brought respect to the U.S. as a major naval power.

U.S. Army troops were sent to the Philippines in August 1898. A **treaty** would now be **negotiated** to decide who would govern the Philippine Islands.

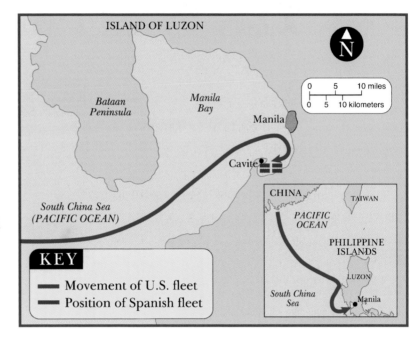

1898 Gazette

- The boats chosen to fight for the U.S. Navy were the USS *Olympia*, the USS *Baltimore*, the USS *Raleigh*, the USS *Boston*, the USS *Concord*, and the USS *Petrel*. There were 1,611 crewmen aboard these six boats.

- The Spanish ships involved in the battle were the *Reina Cristina*, the *Castilla*, the *Don Juan de Austria*, the *Don Antonio de Ulloa*, the *Isla de Cuba*, the *Marqués del Duero*, and the *Isla de Luzon*.

After Action Report

	United States	Spain
Commanders	Commodore George Dewey	Admiral Patricio Montojo
Casualties	9 wounded	161 killed, 210 wounded
Outcome	victory	defeat

JULY	OCTOBER	DECEMBER
7/1 Battle of San Juan Hill 7/1 Battle of Kettle Hill 7/3 Battle of Santiago 7/25 U.S. troops land in Puerto Rico	10/18 Last Spanish troops leave Puerto Rico	

Treaty of Paris

On October 1, 1898, government representatives from the United States and Spain met in Versailles, near Paris, France, to **negotiate** terms for a peace **treaty** to end the Spanish-American War.

Terms of the Treaty

Spain gave up control of Cuba, allowing it to become an independent nation. In addition, Spain gave the islands of Puerto Rico, in the **Caribbean,** and Guam, in the Pacific to the United States. They also gave up control of the Philippine Islands, accepting $20 million in payment from the United States. All Spanish **colonies** involved in the war, except Cuba, would now be under direct control of the government of the United States.

U.S. and Spanish representatives signed the Treaty of Paris on December 10, 1898. The U.S. Senate adopted it on February 6, 1899 by a vote of 52 to 27. President McKinley signed the treaty that same day.

All members of both peace commissions signed the Treaty of Paris, officially ending the Spanish-American War.

The American Peace Commission

- William R. Day, U.S. Secretary of State
- Senator Cushman K. Davis
- Senator William P. Frye
- Senator George Gray
- Whitelaw Reid, a journalist who supported President McKinley and was appointed by him to the Peace Commission.

The Spanish Peace Commission

- Don Eugenio Montero Rios, President of the Spanish Senate
- Jules Cambon, a French diplomat who negotiated on Spain's behalf
- Buenaventura Abarzuza, Senator
- José de Garnica y Diaz, Associate Justice of the Supreme Court
- Wenceslao Ramirez de Villa Urrutia, Envoy Extraordinary
- Rafael Cerero y Saenz, General of the Army

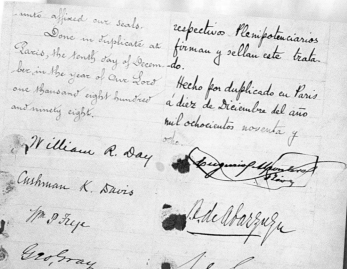

1898	FEBRUARY	APRIL	MAY	JUNE
	2/15 Sinking of the USS *Maine*	4/21 U.S. Navy begins blockade of Cuba 4/23 Spain declares war on the U.S. 4/25 U.S. declares war on Spain	5/1 Battle of Manila Bay	6/22 First landing of U.S. troops at Daiquiri, Cuba 6/22 Capture of Siboney, Cuba 6/24 Battle at Las Guásimas, Cuba

After the War

The Spanish-American War brought changes to all the countries involved in the fighting.

The United States gained new responsibilities with the possession of Puerto Rico, Guam, and the Philippines. They would now be recognized by other countries as a significant power in world affairs. The Spanish lost much of their world empire. The Cubans gained their independence, but struggled to develop an economy that would support their nation. The people of the Philippines were angry that they were not granted independence, but were just placed under the rule of a different nation.

The U.S. would now become a country not just concerned with the problems within its borders, but a country interested in expanding its economic and **political** influence to other parts of the world as well.

This map was made after the Spanish-American War. The U.S. now needed to include all countries that were under its control on its maps. As a result, the U.S. also started to become more involved in affairs outside of the country.

1898 Gazette

The Filipino natives welcomed the help of the United States to win their freedom from Spain. However, they did not welcome the idea that they would now be under the political control of the United States. They wanted to be free and form their own government. Fighting would begin between Filipino natives and the United States soon after peace was reached with Spain.

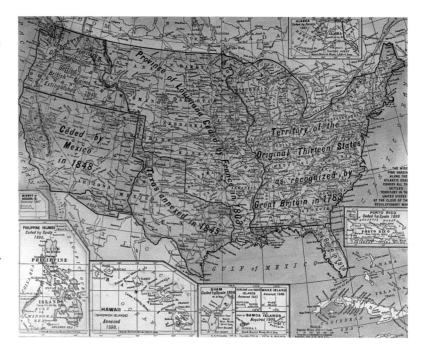

JULY	OCTOBER	DECEMBER
7/1 Battle of San Juan Hill 7/1 Battle of Kettle Hill 7/3 Battle of Santiago 7/25 U.S. troops land in Puerto Rico	10/18 Last Spanish troops leave Puerto Rico	12/10 Treaty of Paris is signed

29

Glossary

artillery   cannons

Asiatic Squadron   group of U.S. Navy ships that patrolled the Pacific Ocean

blockade   to position ships to prevent supplies or other ships from entering a port

brigade   group of soldiers

campaign   military mission

Caribbean   area of the Atlantic Ocean bordered on the north and the east by the West Indies, on the west by Central America, and on the south by South America

cavalry   soldiers who rode horses

Civil War   war fought in the United States from 1861 to 1865 between the Union (North) and Confederate (South) states over issues of slavery and states' rights

colony   territory settled by people from other countries who still had loyalty to those other countries. The word *colonist* is used to describe a person who lives in a colony. The word *colonial* is used to describe things related to a colony.

Congress   men who represented the individual states in the U.S. government, either in the House of Representatives or the Senate

counterattack   attack made in return for another attack

entrenched   position dug into a hillside or area to provide shelter from gunfire and to strengthen an army's defense

flagship   ship that the leader of a group of ships sails on

fleet   group of ships

force   group of soldiers

fortify   to protect

front   place where fighting is happening between enemy forces

harbor   place along the coastline that provides protection for ships

infantry   foot soldiers

intercept   to take while on its way from one person to another

jingo   person who is in favor of their country going to war

land battery   group of cannons on land used to protect cities or forts

malaria   disease with severe chills and fever caused by the bite of mosquitoes that carry the disease

maneuver   planned movement

Medal of Honor   highest military decoration given to members of U.S. armed forces for bravery in combat

negotiate   to try to come to an agreement between two or more people or groups

politics   government affairs

reinforcements   troops brought to help an army under attack

resolution   to work out, or solve a problem

shore battery   group of cannons near the water used to protect a city or harbor

supply depot   building used to store materials

treaty   agreement

Further Reading

Collins, Mary. *The Spanish-American War.* Danbury, Conn.: Children's Press, 1998.

McNeese, Tim. *Remember the Maine!: The Spanish-American War Begins.* Greensboro, N.C.: Morgan Reynolds, Inc., 2001.

Wukovitz, John F. *The Spanish-American War.* Farmington Hills, Mich.: Gale Group, 2001.

Historical Places to Visit

Fort De Soto Park
3500 Pinellas Bayway
Tierra Verde, Florida 33715-2528
Visitor information: (727) 582-2267
An island at the entrance to Tampa Bay, this park has a display of seacoast artillery from the Spanish-American War.

The Navy Museum
Washington Navy Yard
Building 76
805 Kidder Breese SE
Washington, D.C. 20374-5060
Visitor information: (202) 433-4882
This museum, which presents an overview of the history of the U.S. Navy, includes exhibits on the Navy's activities during the Spanish-American War.

San Juan National Historic Site
Fort San Cristobal
Norzagaray Street
San Juan 00901
Puerto Rico
Visitor information: (787) 729-6777
Maintained by the National Park Service, a scale model of this Spanish-built fort, the site of a battle between the U.S. Navy and harbor cannons from the fort during the Spanish-American War, is on display.

U.S. Naval Academy, Armel-Leftwich Visitor Center
52 King George Street (Gate 1)
Annapolis, Maryland 21402
Visitor information: (410) 263-6933
The United States Naval Academy was established in 1845 to prepare young men and women to become professional officers in the U.S. Navy and Marine Corps. The visitor center features interactive exhibits, pictorial displays, and guided tours on the history and traditions of the Naval Academy.

Index